D1312959

Healing the Human Spirit

Ruth Hawkey

New Wine Press

New Wine Press
PO Box 17
Chichester
West Sussex PO20 6YB
England

Scripture quotations are taken from The Amplified Bible. Old
Testament copyright © 1965, 1987 by the Zondervan
Corporation. The Amplified New Testament copyright © 1958,
1987 by the Lockman Foundation. Used by permission.

ISBN: 1 874367 45 0

Typeset by CRB Associates, Norwich
Printed in England by Clays Ltd, St Ives plc.

Contents

Preface

According to the Scriptures man is a tripartite being, which means that he has been created with three parts to his nature: body, soul and spirit. Saint Paul writing to the church at Thessalonica says:

> *'May the God who gives us peace make you holy in every way and keep your whole being – spirit, soul, and body – free from every fault at the coming of our Lord Jesus Christ.'*
>
> (1 Thessalonians 5:23)

and the writer to the Hebrews confirms the three-fold nature of man:

> *'The word of God is alive and active, sharper than any double-edged sword. It cuts all the way through, to where soul and spirit meet, to where joints and marrow come together.'*
>
> (Hebrews 4:12)

5

However, whilst there are a number of books available concerned with the needs of the body and soul, there are not many which deal with the functions and wounding of the human spirit. There is a great deal of literature available concerned with ministering into the physical, emotional and deliverance needs of a person, but very little about ministering into the broken, imprisoned or crushed spirit. This would seem to show that in this area, there is a marked lack of knowledge in the Body of Christ. This is very regrettable, especially when you consider that a person's spirit is the most vital part of their being. In fact, as I hope to show later, without the human spirit functioning properly, the body and the soul cannot.

Many people are walking around today with an apparently healthy body and soul, but with deep inner pain in their spirits. A number of these, after hearing my teaching on the subject on various training courses asked for it to be transcribed into written form. This booklet is the result. I hope that the following teaching will help us to recognise the nature of the human spirit; how it functions; what causes it to become wounded and how to minister God's healing.

Chapter 1

The Origin and Nature
of the Human Spirit

The Origin of the Human Spirit

There are a number of basic questions concerning the origin, nature and work of the human spirit which we need to answer before we can begin to consider how the human spirit becomes wounded.

– What is the human spirit?
– Where does it come from?
– What is its purpose?
– Do we communicate with our spirit and if so how?

Whilst some of these questions are unanswerable, others are certainly within our reach, with the answers, I believe, being deeply rooted in God's word. I want us therefore to look at the scriptural evidence for the work and nature of the human spirit, before we look at how it becomes damaged. I will then give some pointers as to the way of ministering the healing love of Jesus into these wounds.

The first question to be asked would seem to be the most basic and the most obvious, as well as the most important. 'What is the source of the human spirit?' Or in other words, 'where does the human spirit come from?' The answer, as far as Scripture is concerned, is that our spirits come from God Himself. The prophet Zechariah tells us:

> *'Thus says the Lord, Who ... forms the spirit of man within him.'* (Zechariah 12:1)

Just as God breathed the spirit into Adam in the beginning:

> *'Then the Lord God formed man from the dust of the ground and breathed into his nostrils the breath or spirit of life,'* (Genesis 2:7)

so He forms the human spirit within each one of us.

The question then is: 'How does the human spirit get within man? Does God personally breathe the breath of life into each person in the womb?' It seems unlikely, but the answer, I'm afraid, is that we really don't know! As Ecclesiastes writes:

> *'As you know not what is the way of the wind, or how the spirit comes to the bones in the womb of a pregnant woman, even so you know not the work of God, Who does all.'* (Ecclesiastes 11:5)

What he is saying is that we are completely in the dark as to how the human spirit becomes part of a person. A number of scientists have speculated as to how it might happen, but the truth is that at this precise moment, we have to agree with Ecclesiastes. We honestly don't know. However what we do know is that our spirits come from God and will eventually return to God who gave them.

It is interesting to note that the writer of the book of Proverbs describes the human spirit as the:

> *'lamp of the Lord, searching all his innermost parts,'*　　　　　　　　(Proverbs 20:2)

and John, in his gospel, states that Jesus is the:

> *'true Light (was then) coming into the world (the genuine, perfect, steadfast Light) that illumines every person.'*　　　　　(John 1:9)

It is as though Jesus Christ puts a flicker of light into each person as they are conceived, which then becomes their human spirit.

The Nature of the Human Spirit

We may not understand how or when we receive our human spirit but we do know that each one of us has one, as well as a body and a soul. It is that part of us which makes us completely different from every other person; the essential 'you', which is totally unique and special. That part of you which 'speaks' with others in a very deep and meaningful way. As you are probably aware, communication between individuals can take place on a number of different levels. We can communicate simply with our body: through our voices, facial expressions or touch; through our souls on an emotional level, by a sharing of our minds, or a combination of these methods. We also communicate through our spirits, that inner part of us that reaches out to other human beings on a much deeper level than through mere verbal, emotional or tactile expression.

Most of us will have some understanding of the nature of the soul area: our mind with which we think and reason; our emotions with which we feel and respond; our will with which we make decisions. We probably have an even greater understanding of our body and how that works, but what do we understand about the functions of our human spirit?

We have seen that, according to Scripture, God gives to every person who enters the human race a human spirit. This in itself raises a number of important questions. For example:
- What is the nature of the human spirit?
- What is its purpose?
- How does it function?

The Bible teaches us that we are made in the image of God. That our nature 'images' God's nature. In the Amplified Bible the word 'US', is in capital letters:

> *'Let Us (Father, Son and Holy Spirit) make mankind in Our image.'*   (Genesis 1:26)

The Triune God is at work here, creating man after Their Own image, and springing from that discussion amongst the Godhead, that part of us which we call our human spirit took on the shape of the third person of the Trinity, the Holy Spirit. In other words our human spirit was created as a 'reflection', or 'image' of the Holy Spirit. The Father then implanted in man that part of the image of the Godhead (the Holy Spirit) which in man became known as the human spirit. Our human spirit 'images' the Holy Spirit and we need to look at the work and nature of the Holy Spirit in Scripture to see how it happens.

The Nature of the Holy Spirit

To understand then the **nature** of the **human spirit** we need to consider the **nature** of the **Holy Spirit**. Assuming that the imaging process takes place, what is true of the Holy Spirit will also, to a greater or lesser extent, be true of the human spirit. In Scripture the Holy Spirit's **nature** is defined by His different job functions, both primary and secondary. By primary, I mean the main role of the Holy Spirit, upon which the secondary roles rest and depend.

Chapter 2

The Primary Function of the Holy Spirit

The primary function of the Holy Spirit is to communicate life. As we read and study the Scriptures, we see that this is His main role. From Genesis to Revelation the word of God is full of examples of the Holy Spirit being the one who brings Life:

> *'The Spirit of God was moving (hovering, brooding) over the face of the waters.'* (Genesis 1:2)

Brooding, like a mother ready to bring forth life: which, in this instance, was the creation of the world. Another birth situation is recorded by the disciple Luke concerning the coming of Jesus. Luke 1:31 tells of the Angel Gabriel visiting Mary to tell her she was going to give birth to the Son of God. Mary quite rightly asks

> *'How can this be, since I have no ... husband?'*
> (Luke 1:34)

The answer which was given to her was:

'The Holy Spirit shall come upon you.'
(Luke 1:35)

The Angel Gabriel simply states that the Holy Spirit would bring life into Mary's womb; the very life of the second person of the Godhead: Jesus Christ, the Son of God.

Of course the prime example of the Holy Spirit as the Life-giver is that it is He who communicates the life of God into man's spirit. Scripture affirms that because of man's sin, our human spirits are dead towards God and therefore can have no living relationship with Him. The lines of communication are closed and Jesus says that without the Holy Spirit bringing life into our spirits, we can never come alive to God. We need to have our spirits reborn through the life-giving work of the Holy Spirit, in order to become a child of the Father, a member of God's family. Consider Jesus' discourse in John's Gospel with Nicodemus about the absolute necessity of being born of the Spirit:

> *'Jesus answered, I assure you, most solemnly I tell you, that unless a person is born again (anew, from above) he cannot ever see (know, be acquainted with, and experience) the Kingdom of God.'* (John 3:5)

Thus we can only enter the Kingdom of God when our spirit is brought to life by the Holy Spirit,

14

otherwise we remain dead in our trespasses and sins. Through the Fall man died spiritually and the communication channels between God and man were broken. The Holy Spirit clears those communication barriers and brings our human spirit back to life:

'It is the Spirit who gives life.'   (John 6:63)

However, it is even more glorious than that! He not only touches our spirit and brings it alive, but through His work, Christ actually indwells, permeates and makes His home within our human spirits:

'Christ within and among you, the Hope of (realizing the) Glory.'   (Colossians 1:27)

This communication of life by the Holy Spirit is meant to be an ongoing process. We worship God with our spirit, and as we do so the Holy Spirit delights in pouring God's Life into us, life which brings refreshment, joy and vigour. For a number of years we ministered to people who had experienced difficulty with worshipping God, entering into His presence, or with 'knowing' Him as Father. It was assumed that it was an emotional problem, and that because of past bad parenting, they had developed a wrong view of God as a Father and therefore couldn't relate to Him in a right manner. So we would teach them the true picture of God as revealed in Scripture and through

Jesus; we would pray into their past hurt and pain and lead them into repentance and forgiveness and we would minister inner healing, but this was a largely unsuccessful ministry! The reason was that we were praying in the wrong area. We assumed the problem was in the soul, that is in the emotions, when really the problem was in the human spirit. We were led to the passage in Romans 8:15, 16:

'For (the Spirit which) you have now received (is) not a spirit of slavery (to put you once more in bondage to fear, but you have received the Spirit of adoption (the Spirit producing sonship) in (the bliss of) which we cry, Abba (Father)! Father! The Spirit Himself (thus) testifies together with our own spirit (assuring us) that we are children of God.'

The Holy Spirit witnesses with our spirit, not with our emotions! That is where true life-giving communication takes place. As the writer of John's gospel puts it:

'God is a Spirit (a spiritual Being) and those who worship Him must worship Him in spirit and in truth.' (John 4:24)

That is why in worship it is possible to be feeling very low emotionally, to be grief stricken or depressed, and still come into the presence of God and begin to worship with your spirit. That is the reason why God can command that we praise Him in all circumstances, because it is not reliant on how we feel but on our spirit's determination.

The Primary Function of the Human Spirit

Just as the Holy Spirit's primary job function is to communicate life to the human spirit, so in a like manner the human spirit's job function is to communicate life to our own body and soul. In fact when the human spirit ceases to do this and departs, **all** life departs and the body dies. This is why I refer to it as the primary role of the human spirit. The writer James affirms:

> *'the human body apart from the spirit is life-less...'* (James 2:26)

So when the human spirit returns to God and ceases feeding life to the body and soul then, of course, the body dies and returns to the dust. As Ecclesiastes 12:7 puts it:

> *'Then shall the dust (out of which God made man's body) return to the earth as it was, and the spirit shall return to God Who gave it.'*

Jesus was so much in command of His spirit that He was able to say, on approaching death:

> *' "Father, into Your hands I commit My spirit!" And with these words, He expired.'*
> (Luke 23:46)

17

He truly chose to die, releasing His own human spirit to the Father. He laid down His life (His spirit), no one took it from Him.

However, it isn't only death that hinders the flow of life from our spirit into our body and soul, there are a number of other causes. I will show in a later chapter, the serious consequences to the rest of our nature when our human spirit is damaged and cannot fulfil this vital, primary, life-giving job function.

As well as supplying life to ourselves, we are also meant to communicate life to one another through our human spirits. God has given us the ability to touch each other not only physically and emotionally, but also with our spirits. Many of us have had the experience of meeting with someone for the very first time and feeling that we have known, and 'know' them, in a very deep way. We may have known other people for years and yet have never really 'known' them in any depth at all. What has happened? The difference is in the life-giving touch of the spirit. The cry of one lady's heart was: 'My husband will share about the news, the weather or the children, but never, never, never, does he share himself.' Their human spirits rarely touched and yet that was what her spirit longed for, and was created to enjoy.

This touching of spirits can be either 'life enhancing', or 'death producing'. Many folk are wounded and damaged in their spirits because they have had death, rather than life, fed into them continually. This is usually by key figures: parents, siblings, teachers, pastors. We may have experienced the situation when someone speaks good words to us with their mouths, but we receive a different message from their spirit.

So the primary function of our human spirit is to receive the Life of God from the Holy Spirit. This may be solely the created life or, as is true for the Christian, would also include the life of the 'new birth' (John 3:16). We then communicate that life to our own body and soul and thus to each other. We will consider in the next chapter the secondary functions of the Holy Spirit and therefore also of the human spirit.

Chapter 3

Secondary Functions of the Spirit – Part I

As well as the primary function discussed in chapter two, the Holy Spirit has a number of secondary functions. They are secondary, because they rely on the primary (which is communication of life) in order to exist. As we have seen, once this function ceases, so all of the following, secondary functions will cease.

1a. The Holy Spirit as a Communicator of Comfort and Strength

John 14, 15 and 16 talk about the Holy Spirit being a comforter and a strengthener. In these three chapters Jesus speaks continually to the disciples about the Holy Spirit drawing alongside them. He reminds them that He is going to have to leave them, but that they would not be left comfortless. Indeed He assures them:

'I will ask the Father, and He will give you another Comforter (Counsellor, Helper, Intercessor, Advocate, Strengthener and Standby) that He may remain with you forever – The Spirit of Truth.' (John 14:16, 17a)

The Holy Spirit would be a *'parakletos'*, one who would draw alongside as an encourager. What a wonderful promise of strength, help and encouragement is available from the Holy Spirit, not only to the first disciples, but to all those who receive Him. For His job, His purpose, His reason for being, is to come alongside the believer.

1b. The Human Spirit as a Communicator of Comfort and Strength

In like manner, the human spirit, as well as communicating life, is also meant to communicate comfort and strength to the body and soul, as a means of sustaining and encouraging us. When we are weary, disconsolate or grief-stricken it is the job of the human spirit to lift and encourage us. The psalmist knew this when he wrote:

'Why are thou cast down, O my inner self? And why should you moan over me and be disquieted within me? Hope in God.' (Psalm 42:5)

In other words the psalmist is telling the spirit to do its job! Paul reminds us that the human spirit is also meant to encourage and comfort others. He writes that he is full of joy at seeing Titus because:

> *'you have all set his mind at rest, soothing and refreshing his spirit.'*

2a. The Holy Spirit as a Communicator of Truth

The Holy Spirit is the one who reveals the hidden things of God, the one who will communicate the truth of God to man. Isaiah 40:13–14 reminds us that no one can teach God anything or find out what God is like by his own means. Jesus, teaching His disciples this important truth, asserts:

> *'When He, the Spirit of Truth (the Truth – giving Spirit) comes, He will guide you into all Truth.'* (John 16:13)

It is the work of the Holy Spirit to reveal the truth about God. One of the ways in which He does this is through the inspiration of the Scriptures. As Peter asserts in his second letter:

> *'No prophecy of Scripture is (a matter) of any personal or private or special interpretation (loosening, solving). For no prophecy ever originated because some man willed it (to do so – it never came by human impulse), but men spoke from God who were borne along (moved and impelled) by the Holy Spirit.'* (2 Peter 1:20, 21)

This work of the Holy Spirit is for a specific purpose. 2 Timothy 3:16, 17 says:

'Every Scripture is God-breathed (given by His inspiration) and profitable for instruction, for reproof and conviction of sin, for correction of error and discipline in obedience, (and) for training in righteousness (in holy living, in conformity to God's will in thought, purpose and action).'

The Holy Spirit also reveals the mind of God to the believer. As Paul writes to the Corinthians, the wisdom and blessings of God have now been revealed:

'God has unveiled and revealed them by and through His Spirit, for the (Holy) Spirit searches diligently, exploring and examining everything, even sounding the profound and bottomless things of God (the divine counsels and things hidden and beyond man's scrutiny).'

(1 Corinthians 12:10)

The place where the Holy Spirit reveals truth, to the individual, is within his human spirit. This is where guidance is received, and because we are all open to error this will need testing by more mature Christians and lined up continually with the Scriptures. The same is true of the gifts of the Holy Spirit. Words of knowledge, wisdom, prophecy, interpretation of tongues etc., are all placed in the human spirit by the Holy Spirit, and will need to be judged and discerned by the Body of Christ. We are encouraged to test everything especially with regard to prophecy, where we have been told to:

> *'pay attention and weigh and discern what is said.'* (1 Corinthians 14:29)

However, testing everything doesn't mean that we test the truth of God with our minds alone, and if the gift does not line up with commonsense we disregard it. This can often happen with the gifts of the Spirit. Our mind can become the 'censor' of the human spirit. We receive a gift from the Holy Spirit, maybe a word of knowledge concerning someone for whom we are praying. The Holy Spirit has placed that 'truth' into our spirits, in order for us to communicate it into the life of the person in need. However our mind moves forward into action. We think: 'That cannot be a true word of knowledge, it doesn't make sense,' or 'That cannot possibly be a prophetic word, it is too ridiculous.' This censorship of the mind over the spirit means that we do not speak out the truth which the Holy Spirit has given to us. In other words we:

> *'quench (suppress or subdue) the (Holy) Spirit.'* (1 Thessalonians 5:19)

We need to constantly remember that:

> *'the natural, nonspiritual man does not accept or welcome or admit into his heart the gifts and*

> *teachings and revelations of the Spirit of God,*
> *for they are folly (meaningless nonsense) to*
> *him; and he is incapable of knowing them (of*
> *progressively recognizing, understanding, and*
> *becoming better acquainted with them) because*
> *they are spiritually discerned and estimated and*
> *appreciated.'* (1 Corinthians 2:14)

We are all in the process of having our carnal nature changed into the fully spiritual being, who has the 'mind of Christ' and until that is accomplished, we need to remember Paul's warning that the 'unspiritual' man cannot understand or judge the 'spiritual'.

2b. The Human Spirit as a Communicator of Truth

Because we 'image' or 'mirror' the Holy Spirit, there is a part of the human spirit whose job function is to reveal truth, truth in the inward parts. It is also the place where we receive our 'knowing' and our 'intuition' about God and others.

> *'For what person perceives (knows and under-*
> *stands) what passes through a man's thoughts*
> *except the man's own spirit within him?'*
> (1 Corinthians 2:11)

This 'knowing' begins even in the womb. Luke records an amazing statement concerning Mary's visit to her cousin Elizabeth, who was six months pregnant. As Mary arrives at her house, Luke says:

> *'when Elizabeth heard Mary's greeting, the baby leaped in her womb,'* (Luke 1:41)

and just in case we didn't receive it the first time, Luke repeats this staggering truth as Elizabeth cries out:

> *'For behold, the instant the sound of your salutation reached my ears, the baby in my womb leaped for joy.'* (Luke 1:44)

Why was the baby leaping? Because there was an intuitive 'knowing' by John the Baptist, whilst in the womb of his mother, that he was in the presence of Jesus the Son of God, who at that moment in time, was within the womb of Mary. Where did John receive this revelation? I believe that he received it from the Holy Spirit who placed it into his human spirit. Thus the baby leapt for joy as Elizabeth was:

> *'filled with and controlled by the Holy Spirit.'* (Luke 1:41b)

He (the Holy Spirit), prompted her to speak the words which were an enormous encouragement and strength to Mary at that very difficult time:

> *'Blessed (favoured of God) above all other women are you! And blessed (favoured of God) is the Fruit of your womb.'*   (Luke 1:42)

These words, which were spoken from Elizabeth's spirit straight into Mary's spirit, caused her in turn to proclaim:

> *'My spirit rejoices in God my Saviour.'*
> (Luke 1:47)

An amazing example of the job function of the Holy Spirit working with the job function of the human spirit, revealing and communicating encouragement, life and truth both to the person, and through that person, into the spirit of another, in this case Mary the mother of Jesus.

This intuitive knowing or revealing aspect of the human spirit continues throughout a person's life. Peter knew in his spirit that Jesus was:

> *'the Christ, the Son of the living God.'*
> (Matthew 16:16)

We are told that this was a revelation to him from the Father in heaven; in other words from the Holy Spirit into Peter's spirit. We 'know' others and 'know' the truth about others through our spirits. Someone may speak pleasant, kind and seemingly upbuilding words to you, but in your spirit you are reading a different message. You feel uneasy. Why? Because with their words they are saying one thing, but in their spirits they are saying something totally different and you are reading their spirit. They speak or communicate 'life' with their lips, but 'death' with their spirit.

3a. The Holy Spirit as the One who Convicts

It is also the Holy Spirit's job function to bring men and women under conviction of sin and of their need of a Saviour:

> *'And when He comes, He will convict and convince the world and bring demonstration to it about sin.'*   (John 16:8)

It is impossible for a preacher or an evangelist to convict a person of their need of the Saviour. That is the job function of the Holy Spirit. We can bring them under condemnation; only He can bring them to conviction. Those involved with the great revivals knew the truth of this and leant heavily upon this aspect of the Holy Spirit's work. Most Christians are all too aware of the convicting work of the Holy Spirit within their lives and it would seem that the nearer a person draws to God, the more conscious they become of their sin.

3b. The Human Spirit as the One who Convicts

In a similar manner the human spirit is also meant

to convict a person (through their conscience) of right and wrong. If it is fulfilling its job function then the spirit keeps the body and soul in line with God's law, which Scripture says is written in every one's heart:

> *'They (the Gentiles) show that the essential requirements of the Law are written in their hearts and are operating there, with which their consciences (sense of right and wrong) also bear witness.'* (Romans 2:15)

So, if we have the law of God within our hearts and one of the functions of our spirit is that of bringing conviction, then we have no excuse for sin when we stand before God, whether we are Christians or not. It is possible, though, for the conscience to be rendered inactive, because it has become hardened against God's law:

> *'Today, if you would hear His voice and when you hear it, do not harden your hearts.'*
> (Hebrews 4:7)

We need to constantly allow the Holy Spirit to convict us of any hardening towards sin. We also need to allow Him to examine us as to whether our conscience has become defiled and therefore cannot fulfil this very important role of acting like a 'spiritual policeman'. We shall look in a later chapter as to the reasons for a defiled spirit, and how to minister cleansing and wholeness in order for our spirits to become sensitive and so fulfil this very important role.

4a. The Holy Spirit as a Creator

Another function of the Holy Spirit is that of being involved with acts of creation. We have already noted that the Holy Spirit was present at the creation of the world, as He worked alongside the Father and the Son, in bringing into being the universe as we know it. Job goes further and affirms that the Holy Spirit was not only involved in the creation of the world, He was actually involved in the creation of 'me'.

> *'The Spirit of God has made me.'*   (Job 33:4)

Job was no doubt basing that conviction on the story in Genesis 2, where it is written that God:

> *'formed man from the dust of the ground and breathed into his nostrils the breath or spirit of life, and man became a living being.'*
>
> (Genesis 2:7)

This is very reminiscent of the time when Jesus appeared to his disciples after the resurrection and:

> *'breathed on them and said to them, "Receive (admit) the Holy Spirit!"'*   (John 20:22)

Here we are seeing the Holy Spirit present and involved in a new creation, which was ultimately fulfilled at Pentecost; the creation of the Church, the Body of Christ.

4b. The Human Spirit as a Creator

To a lesser extent the human spirit is also meant to be a vehicle for creativity, the difference being that our creativity is a 'secondary creativity', relying and drawing inspiration from God's creation. Nevertheless, with that proviso, there is a function of man's spirit which is able to create. The majority of inspirational and beautiful music was created first in the human spirit of the composer and then flowed out of his spirit onto the page. That is why when we are listening to a wonderful composition, we are moved in our 'spirit'. The music, which began in another spirit, is speaking to our spirit. The same could be said about beautiful and moving works of art and explains, to some extent, why men and women will give anything to possess a certain picture, book or artefact. They are reaching out in their spirits to that which was first created in another human spirit.

This creative function, I believe, is also the reason why some people have a deep desire and longing to be out walking on the mountains; crossing deep valleys or simply standing and beholding a rushing mighty waterfall. They are desirous of feeding that creative area of their human spirit. Such manifestations of nature are to the spirit what a drink of clear cold water would be to a dry and thirsty man.

Chapter 4

Secondary Functions of the Spirit –
Part II

5a. The Holy Spirit as the One who Empowers

'But truly I (Micah) am full of power of the Spirit of the Lord.' (Micah 3:8)

The Old Testament is full of examples of men and women who were empowered by the Holy Spirit: Elisha (2 Kings 2:14), Samson (Judges 14:6) and Gideon (Judges 6:34), to name but a few. The Holy Spirit is the empowerer, the one who strengthens the Body of Christ. Indeed Jesus warns His disciples not to go running around in their own strength, but to wait in Jerusalem, in order that they may receive the power of the Holy Spirit. He promises His disciples and future believers:

'you shall receive power (ability, efficiency, and might) when the Holy Spirit has come upon you,' (Acts 1:8)

and we need only to read the book of Acts to see how much and how effectively the Holy Spirit empowered the early Church. History confirms that He has continued his work down the ages, empowering and strengthening each new generation of the Church.

5b. The Human Spirit as the One who Empowers

Similarly the human spirit is meant to provide power and strength to the body and soul.

> *'The strong spirit of a man sustains him in bodily pain or trouble.'*   (Proverbs 18:14)

The stronger our human spirits are, the more able they will be to fulfil this role. Many heroic tales are told of people who have supernatural strength under impossible circumstances. How do they do it, we ask? I suggest one reason might be that their spirit is performing this function in a superhuman way. Or consider those going through a very difficult time with many friends praying for them. They feel strong and able to cope much better than they ever imagined. What is happening? I suggest that those who are praying are, in their spirit, strengthening the body and soul of their friend in need.

A lady wrote to me recently concerning the help her friends were to her as she was going through a very difficult time. Her marriage was not good, her sons were verbally abusing her, she felt abandoned by almost everyone and was experiencing great rejection. She says: 'I was unable to get up off my couch. I could not even pray. I had friends who took my needs to the Lord. As long as they prayed I could function, but when they stopped, I could feel my strength being drained away.'

What was happening? I believe that they were fulfilling this role of pouring strength into her spirit through their prayers. The Holy Spirit was interceding for her through them and thus her body and soul were strengthened until she herself was strong enough in spirit to pray for herself.

The question which then arises is: 'How is the human spirit strengthened in order for it to fulfil this very important function?' I would suggest that for the Christian, there are a number of ways. As we have seen, we can be strengthened through the prayers of our friends in the Body of Christ; through the prayers of Jesus, who is always interceding for each one of us at the right hand of God; through worship; through reading God's Word and through speaking in tongues. Paul writes that this 'edifies' the Christian, it builds him up. The most vital way for our spirit to be strengthened however is through the prayers of the Holy Spirit who:

> *'Himself goes to meet our supplication and pleads in our behalf with unspeakable yearnings and groanings too deep for utterance.'*

> (Romans 8:26)

I would also suggest that when the Holy Spirit prays for us the job function of the Holy Spirit and the job function of the human spirit are linked together, like cogs in a wheel. We then draw from Him the power, strength and comfort which we need. It was said of both John the Baptist and Jesus that they:

> *'became strong in spirit.'*
>
> (Luke 1:80a; Luke 2:40a)

I believe this was through the empowering of their spirits by the Holy Spirit.

6a. The Holy Spirit as a Facilitator

The Holy Spirit is also a facilitator, the means by which God's plans are translated into action. For example, as we have seen, the Holy Spirit was the one who brought into being God's plans for the creation of the world:

> *'The earth was without form and an empty waste, and darkness was upon the face of the very great deep. The Spirit of God was moving (hovering, brooding) over the face of the water;'*
>
> (Genesis 1:2b)

and also of the Incarnation:

> *'His mother Mary had been promised in marriage to Joseph, before they came together,*

she was found to be pregnant (through the power) of the Holy Spirit.' (Matthew 1:18)

The Holy Spirit enabled the work of Jesus to be so effective:

'But if it is by the Spirit of God that I drive out demons, then the Kingdom of God has come upon you.' (Matthew 12:28)

Jesus only began His public ministry after He was baptized with the Holy Spirit (Luke 3:22). Indeed Luke tells us that it was the Holy Spirit who controlled Jesus and led Him into the wilderness (Luke 4:1) after which:

'Jesus went back full of and under the power of the (Holy) Spirit into Galilee.' (Luke 4:14)

The Holy Spirit was also the facilitator who enabled Jesus to rise from the dead. According to Romans 8:11:

'And if the Spirit of Him Who raised up Jesus from the dead dwells in you, (then) He Who raised up Christ Jesus from the dead will also restore to life your mortal (short-lived, perishable) bodies through His Spirit Who dwells in you.'

Isn't that wonderful? It is the Holy Spirit who will raise us to life, just as He did with Jesus.

6b. The Human Spirit as a Facilitator

I would suggest that our human spirits also 'mirror' or 'image' the Holy Spirit in being facilitators of God's purposes, to a lesser extent. It is, of course, only the Holy Spirit's work within and through the human spirit that brings in the Kingdom of God. Nevertheless we, as part of the Body of Christ, have a role to play, which is to be led by the Holy Spirit and allow Him to work though us (that is through our spirit) in order that we might 'work the works of God'. It is in our spirits that we receive the fruit and the gifts of the Holy Spirit, which God means to flow through us, in order to bring evangelism, healing and deliverance to a needy world.

So in summary, we can see that the human spirit mirrors or images the nature of the Holy Spirit and thus has similar primary and secondary job functions, the primary functions being: to receive life in the human spirit via the Holy Spirit; to communicate with and worship the Creator; to communicate and sustain the life of the body and soul; to communicate and interact with others. I call these the primary functions because without communication of life to the body (physical) and to the spirit (spiritual), death reigns and the other functions cease or are limited. Therefore the other functions rely to some greater or lesser extent upon the primary function.

The secondary functions of the human spirit are: to comfort and encourage my body and soul and that of others; to understand and know the things of God and man, through revelation or intuition; to bring conviction through the conscience; to take part in creative activities; to empower and strengthen my body and soul and that of others; to allow the spirit to be used by the Holy Spirit to facilitate the plans of God and so assist in establishing the Kingdom of God.

Chapter 5

A Model to Meet the World

I would like to suggest to you a new way of approaching the world, which for the Christian who wants to be led by the Holy Spirit is really the only way to live. The suggestion is that we ought to be meeting other people and situations not primarily with our bodies and souls but with our spirits. What do I mean by that? Paul writes to the Christians at Thessalonica that we are spirit, soul and body (1 Thessalonians 5:23). Very often we turn that around and quote it as 'body, soul and spirit', because that is our experience of approaching the world. We meet people with our bodies first, then our souls (mind, emotions and will) and then maybe, just maybe, we touch spirits. However, as Paul knew, we are first and foremost spiritual beings who need to learn how to approach others 'spirit first'.

In order to put that into practice we need to change our thinking and follow the lead of Jesus who continually met people and situations 'spiritually' first. For example He was already spiritually attuned at the age of twelve, when He was found:

> *'in My Father's house and (occupied) about My Father's business?'* (Luke 2:49)

He spiritually read the situation of the woman taken in adultery and responded accordingly, to give an accurate summing up of the universality of sin; He was spiritually aware of the pain and wounding in the woman who had bled for twelve years and dealt not only with her physical problem, but her inner isolation and unrest as well.

> *'Daughter, your faith (your confidence and trust in Me) has made you well! Go (enter) into peace (untroubled, undisturbed well-being).'*
> (Luke 8:43–48)

Jesus was truly:

> *'led by the Spirit of God.'* (Romans 8:14)

For us to do likewise the human spirit needs to be in 'spiritual alignment' with the Holy Spirit. He will then feed life; comfort and encouragement; truth and knowledge; conviction of right and wrong; strength and power into our human spirit, and because we have aligned our spirit with Him, we take these attributes and through the same job functions of our spirit, we feed them into our own body and soul and out into the world. Thus we find that we are 'led' by the Holy Spirit. He enables us to meet people spirit to spirit and as the water of life flows out of our 'bellies', so others are touched and changed by Him.

The only drawback to this way of living is that it makes you very vulnerable, especially if you are a sensitive person. This is because when you open your spirit (your 'inner being') to someone else, you risk your spirit being trampled on. In the Jewish Temple the Holy of Holies is on the inside, the Inner Sanctuary next and then the Outer Court. The Holy of Holies is like the human spirit. It is that inner part of a person which needs to be guarded and treasured, but ready to be revealed to those who wish to draw near and meet, spirit to spirit.

When the human spirit has been brought alive to God, indwelt by the Spirit of God and functioning the way He intended, then we live a life which is full and satisfying. The problem arises, however, when the spirit becomes sick and the functions become impaired. There are a lot of people who are not only damaged in their emotions, or in their bodies, but they also carry deep wounds in their spirits. Nelson Mandela returned to visit Robben Island where he was in jail for nineteen years. The trip came on the fourth anniversary of his release from prison. As he shared some of the memories of those times, the pain inevitably seeped through. 'Wounds that can't be seen are more painful than those that can be seen and cured by a doctor,' said

Mr Mandela. 'One of the saddest moments in my life in prison was the death of my mother. The next shattering experience was the death of my eldest son in a car accident.' He was forbidden from attending either funeral. Such wounds go deep.

The questions which then arise are:
- How does our spirit become sick?
- What are the causes of damage?
- How does this damage affect the functions of the spirit?
- What are the symptoms and what are the remedies for a sick spirit?

In other words 'How do we minister into this vital area?'

Chapter 6

Areas of Damage – A Timid Spirit

Now that we have seen the origin, nature and function of the human spirit, let us consider what happens when it becomes sick or damaged in any way. In order to do that we will look at the various kinds of damage that may occur.

A Timid and Fearful Spirit

Many people limp through their lives with what I have called a 'timid spirit'. They appear to be frightened of every new situation and even of life itself, although as Scripture reminds us:

> *'God did not give us a spirit of timidity (of cowardice, of craven and cringing and fawning fear).'* (2 Timothy 1:7)

Whilst some people suffer from varied emotional fears, for example fear of travel, fear of the dark or fear of spiders, those with a 'timid spirit' suffer non-specific but a rather generalised, all-pervasive fear and anxiety about life itself. This goes much deeper, springing not from their emotions, but from their spirits.

What are the hallmarks of a person with a timid spirit? They will be the kind of person who will continually need lots of reassurance and love. You may feed much affection into them, but this will quickly disappear down a bottomless hole. They will often draw back from new situations, desiring to keep in the background as much as possible. One lady we shared with and ministered to was a church organist. Every Sunday she had to face the congregation as she made her way to the organ to play for the service. It felt, in her own words, 'like dying a thousand deaths'. The distance she had to walk was approximately six metres, but to her it was the equivalent of climbing Mount Everest. Her timid spirit shrivelled up at the thought of it, and she felt like taking flight physically. It was sheer grit and determination which made her fulfil what she saw as her duty.

Very often they will have a guarded approach to life and won't come out to meet you. You may make contact with their outer being, but they will never reveal their soul or their inner spirit. They are unsure as to whether life, or people, can ever really be good to them or can be trusted not to wound them further. They fear and expect the worst. They live with the expectation that life will hit them in the back and knock them flat on their face. They may be the kind of person who has a high degree of sensitivity to criticism, which they see when none is intended, and read into other people's body language unspoken disapproval of themselves. They keep their timid spirit closed and locked against others, because they are terrified that they are going to be hurt and wounded even more than they have been. They are like the little canary who refuses to fly, because it fears that flying will lead to death.

Causes of a Timid Spirit

Usually the root of a timid spirit will be found in some trauma in early life, for example like the child who was continually sick at birth. After a number of x-rays and examinations, it was discovered that she was born with her intestines the wrong way round, which was why she couldn't digest her food. The child had an emergency operation when she was three weeks old and the surgeon very wisely warned the parents that 'new situations' might cause the child some fear and anxiety. He was right. She, as a result of that trauma, became 'timid' in her spirit. Thankfully the Lord, over the years, has brought a great measure of healing to her.

The traumas could include any pre- or post-birth experiences. If a pregnant woman receives a terrible shock whilst carrying her baby in the womb, the baby may pick up the timidity of the mother in its own spirit. A very difficult and traumatic birth could be another source. Sometimes timidity of spirit can be the result of the death of a parent at a young age, an accident or separation from the parents for any reason. In fact whenever security is perceived to be removed from the child, it can have this adverse reaction in its young spirit.

It is also possible for there to be a generational problem, where there may be a tendency for timidity of spirit to be passed down the family line. This can usually be traced to some incident in the past which has had a deep and lasting effect upon the family. One gentleman we ministered to had a great grandfather who had been in a violent argument with a neighbour and was consequently murdered. The subsequent men in the family all suffered from timidity of spirit.

Functions Impaired

The functions of the human spirit which are impaired here are: communication with others which becomes very inhibited; and an inability to comfort or empower their own body and soul, therefore leaving them unable to strengthen the spirit and soul of others in need.

Ministering to the Timid Spirit

In every kind of damage to the human spirit, you will need to be aware that the memories and pain which has caused the wounding, will need to be exposed and healed. So we must be continually looking for the root of the wounding. However, for this to be done, the person will need to come to a place of security with you, for they will not share their innermost being until they feel that they can trust you and that you are, indeed, a trustworthy person. This takes time. When you have gained their trust, there are a number of questions which will need to be asked, such as:

- What happened in the past to cause this timidity of spirit?
- Does the timidity show itself in any specific situations, and if so, what are they?
- Did your parents have a similar problem? (Here you are looking for a generational timidity as instanced above.)

Because Satan takes advantage of the dark and wounded places in our lives, we have to be aware that the demonic may also need to be dealt with, if and when it arises. We will take this as understood and therefore not repeat it each time we consider ministering into the wounded spirit.

Once we have discovered the root, we then begin to pray under the guidance of the Holy Spirit, asking Him to bring to the surface any buried traumatic memory and praying through it. We ask that He will be the bridge between the memory and the pain, in order for the hurt, shame or any other emotions to be released to the Lord. We need to specifically release the fear and pray into their spirits the *'shalom'*, the peace of Jesus. We then need to teach the person the importance of being:

> *'transformed (changed) by the (entire) renewal of your mind (by its new deals and its new attitude).'*   (Romans 12:2)

They will need to learn how to work with the Holy Spirit, in order to change their behaviour patterns and attitudes from fear to complete confidence in Him. They need to grasp with their spirit the fact that He is, and will be, their strength and encourager. This comes through a revelation from the Holy Spirit into their spirits, into that 'intuitive' part, which grasps spiritual truth.

Summary

1. Take time to build up **trust** with the person.
2. Always look for the **root** of the 'timidity'.
3. Pray and allow the Holy Spirit to minister into the **roots**.
4. Teach the person the importance of renewing their **mind**.

Chapter 7

Areas of Damage –
An Imprisoned Spirit

Some people are walking around with their human spirit bound and chained, as though it were in a dank, dark, depressing prison. They live within themselves, simply existing in a cage, with iron bars around them. This inhibits freedom and causes their spirit to sink into the gloom of despair and despondency. They never, or rarely, know the joy of fun and laughter, creativity and exuberance. The psalmist knew something of that experience when he cried out that the enemy:

> *'has made me to dwell in dark places as those who have been long dead. Therefore is my spirit overwhelmed and faints within me (wrapped in gloom),'* (Psalm 143:3)

and longs for God to

> *'Bring my life out of prison.'* (Psalm 142:7)

The one with an imprisoned spirit is doubly bound. He is bound by the chains which hold him and the iron bars which inhibit him. The chains I see as the **cause** of his imprisonment, whilst the bars I see as the **result** of that imprisonment.

Causes of an Imprisoned Spirit

Let us consider the chains or causes first. As with the timid spirit, any traumatic situation can imprison the spirit. A lady we ministered to was put straight into an incubator when she was born. (Her mother was seriously ill and needed to be attended to first.) The baby was presumed dead by the doctor and it was some hours, if not a whole day, before they had finished attending to the mother and turned their attention to the baby.

She had been left alone without food or nurture for what must have seemed, to the baby, a very long time. The result was that her spirit, as well as her body, became entrapped in that incubator. She developed an 'imprisoned spirit'. The details of her birth were relayed to her by her mother who affirmed that from the moment she was able to pick her daughter up, she would withdraw and turn away from her.

Because we are spirit, soul and body, any kind of physical or emotional bondage can cause the spirit to become imprisoned too. For example, physical addictions, such as alcohol or drug abuse, anorexia or bulimia will have a repercussion in the spirit.

Any kind of emotional control or domination can have the same result, like the child who, at three years old, waited outside her parent's workplace for them to finish their work shift. She was terrified of moving, standing and feeling like a stone statue, both inside and out, because mother had said, 'Stand there and don't move or the bogey-man will get you!'

If a person has been starved in any way this will have a repercussion in their spirit. The starvation may have been of food (as with the baby placed in the incubator and presumed dead) or of affection, or even protection. Starvation, of any kind, dries up the spirit. Parents who have run a home based on a very strict regime, such as the father who was a sergeant major, both on the parade ground and at home!, will cause the spirit of the child to become very withdrawn and isolated. Sometimes Christians suffering from strict legalism in their church, or very heavy shepherding, will need ministry into their imprisoned spirit, as well as into spiritual abuse. They will have had heavy chains of legalism imposed upon them, from which they will need to be set free.

The Results of an Imprisoned Spirit

Because the one whose spirit is in prison has been badly hurt, they place bars of protection around themselves in order that the hurt will not grow more intense. The iron bars may be many and varied, but in my experience **isolation** is normally one of the key ones. This is usually self-imposed, in that they prefer their own company. 'Nobody is going to get close to me, and I won't allow myself to get close to others' is a description of their inner life. The path of solitude is much more preferable than that of being in fellowship with others, because they do not know how to relate. They are likely to be the 'lone wolf' in your congregation. Linked with this is the iron bar of **control**, in that they like to control their own patch. It makes them feel much safer. Very often they will try to control their families as well. The bar of **legalism** is a life-style which suits the person with an imprisoned spirit and sometimes a Christian will find themselves drawn to a very legalistic fellowship for that very reason.

Denial and **poverty** are the final bars which keep them in prison. They literally feel that they shouldn't have anything good or enjoyable. They are unworthy. The 'bread and water diet', or the 'hair-shirt regime' is all that they are worthy of obtaining. This is not a reasoned, thought out, point of view, it is something that has been seared into their very spirit. They feel guilty if they are enjoying themselves and very quickly find a reason to stop. They must live on the minimum. One lady, who was given lots of beautiful presents by her family for Christmas or birthdays would put them to one side and give them away to others throughout the year. She didn't feel worthy to receive such gifts.

Functions Impaired

For the person with the imprisoned spirit the primary function of communication is seriously impaired. Consider someone trying to communicate through iron bars or, as sometimes happens in a prison, trying to talk through a glass panel. This is how it can feel to the one with their spirit in prison. Often they will feel completely misunderstood or misheard. This is because the communication function is not working properly. Within a marriage, if both partners have imprisoned spirits, they end up not communicating, but shouting at each other, with neither understanding the other!

The secondary function of revelation and intuition is also seriously distorted. They cannot see the world, God, or other people with a right perspective, just as our bodies are distorted if we view ourselves in the funfair mirrors at Blackpool! The creative role is also impaired; it is not free to soar, because it has leaden boots on!

Ministering to the Imprisoned Spirit

First you must look for, and minister into, the reasons and roots of the chains that bind them, asking questions such as:
- What caused your spirit to become so locked away and twisted?
- What prompted that poverty of outlook?
- What caused your joylessness?

The Holy Spirit may give words of knowledge

concerning their past. He may bring into their minds a memory or a picture, which will reveal the source of the problem, like the word of knowledge which was given, concerning a gentleman we were ministering to. The word was 'coffin'. The Holy Spirit used this word to reveal the root of his problem. Evidently, when he was a young child of three, his mother had left him with an uncle for the day. The uncle had become ill during the course of the morning, leaving the young child very frightened and vulnerable. He had spent the major part of the day trying to attract attention by banging on the window or trying to shake his uncle into consciousness. The result was that he felt trapped as though he were in a coffin. What happened to him physically had deep repercussions in his spirit.

After you have discovered the roots of the imprisonment, you will need to pray through them, breaking the chains; the same will need to be done concerning the iron bars, which have been erected to protect them from any more pain. They will need, by an act of their will, to choose to take those iron bars down, repent for trying to protect themselves and choose to allow God to protect them in the future. Each bar will need to be broken specifically, through the power of the Holy Spirit, always being aware that the demonic may be present, for he loves to work in the dark.

The person will come to a point in ministry where they will need to walk out of their prison, just as Lazarus had to choose to *'come forth'*, when Jesus called him out. A lifetime of habit structures will need to be laid to rest. Take time to encourage them to:

> *'be transformed (changed) by the (entire) renewal of your mind,'* (Romans 12:2)

and to alter their behaviour patterns as the Lord points them out. Jesus can call their spirit back to life, but they have to remove the bars and bandages which they have put around their spirit. They need to see that they are a child of God with a right to enjoy life, a right to joy, freedom and creativity.

You will also need to feed and nurture their spirit, little by little replacing what has been missing, fun things as well as spiritual. Good parents automatically feed their child's spirit. It is the first thing mothers do when they feed their baby at the breast. They pour not only food into the baby, but love, pride and joy as well. Just look at the smile on the face of a new mother. This smile and pride increases when father notes the first tooth, the first words, the first faltering, stumbling steps, all filling the heart with joy and bringing that spirit to spirit communication which is so essential to the baby's development. 'You are wonderful.' 'You are the most amazing child that has ever been born.' 'There is no child like our child!' Of course there is a reassessment later! But the child's spirit has been fed and nurtured at a very important stage in its life.

The person with an imprisoned spirit has never known that nurturing of the spirit (not always because of the fault of the parents) but nevertheless is starved on the inside. Such children don't know that they are wonderful, that they are precious and valuable. Someone in the Body of Christ has to be available to feed such truth into their spirits. Remember to give the person permission to enjoy themselves, reminding them that healing may be a slow process, but that as they work with God, gradually they will begin to walk out into a greater freedom, and know the truth which Charles Wesley wrote:

> 'Long my imprisoned spirit lay
> Fast bound in sin and nature's night;
> Thine eye diffused a quickening ray –
> I woke, the dungeon filled with light;
> My chains fell off, my heart was free,
> I rose, went forth, and followed thee.'
>
> (Methodist Hymn Book)

Summary

1. Look for and minister into the **roots**.
2. Lead them in **repentance** for erecting the iron bars.
3. Get them to **choose** to take the iron bars down.
4. **Holy Spirit** led ministry.
5. Remind them that their wrong **habit structures** will need breaking.
6. Feed and **nurture** their spirit.

Chapter 8

Areas of Damage – A Crushed Spirit

The third area of damage to the spirit is that of having a crushed and bruised spirit, or a heavy, burdened and failing spirit. Scripture lays the blame for this on Satan:

> *'He (the enemy) has crushed my life down to the ground.'*　　　　　　(Psalm 143:3)

Some people seem to be continually grieving on the inside. They have very little self-affirmation and almost no self-worth. If you ask such a person what they think about themselves, you will read self-rejection in every sentence of their answer. There will probably be a sense of weariness and despair in their body language. Because their spirit is crushed it cannot do its job function of sustaining, strengthening and encouraging their body and soul. Very often their face will show continual sadness, with tears always near to the surface.

For people with a crushed and heavy spirit, suicide may be constantly on their minds: 'What's the use?' 'What is the point?' 'I might as well give up.' 'I'd be better off dead.' Self-pity may take root, as in the case of Elijah when threatened by Jezebel:

> *'And I, I only, am left, and they seek my life, to destroy it.'*   (1 Kings 19:14b)

Sometimes people who have a crushed spirit will resort to anorexia or bulimia, because the role of supporting and strengthening the body becomes too onerous and the spirit gives up. It begins to seek to destroy that which it is meant to support. The good news, as the prophet Isaiah reminds us, is that God will give:

> *'the garment (expressive) of praise instead of a heavy, burdened, and failing spirit.'*

> (Isaiah 61:3)

Causes of a Crushed Spirit

One of the main causes of a crushed spirit is in-appropriate burden bearing. Many people are called upon to walk through life with responsibilities, which are far too onerous for their age or experience, like the little girl whom I taught. She had the responsibility, at the age of five, of getting herself ready for school every morning, her mother being unable or unwilling, to get out of bed because of late nights spent with her friends. However Helen (as I will call her) not only had to feed, wash and dress herself, she also had to do the same for her three year old brother. She was then responsible for taking him to nursery, before making her way, wearily, to school by herself.

Considering her young age, it was not surprising that even then she was showing signs of a crushed, heavy and burdened spirit. Helen had never known protection, only burdens placed upon her. Therefore the natural joy and exuberance of childhood was sadly missing. Her shoulders would be stooped, her face expressive of deep sadness, and it took most of the morning to encourage her to relax and play with her friends.

Any form of manipulation and control from authority figures can cause crushing of the spirit. Teachers may do this unthinkingly, as they place a sensitive child in front of a class and insist on them performing! As well as physically cringing, very often the spirit will cringe too. Harsh leadership or powerful words can bring a crushing of the human spirit, as was the case with Elijah. We see him, in 2 Kings 18, fearlessly calling down the fire of the Lord on the prophets of Baal. In 2 Kings 19, we see him running for his life, because of the threatening words of Jezebel, who sent this message to him:

> *'So let the gods do to me, and more also, if I make not your life as the life of one of them (the Baal prophets who were dead) by this time (tomorrow).'* (1 Kings 19:2)

These words were enough to send Elijah into a spiral of despair. In fact he was so frightened and crushed in spirit that he ran for eighty miles, until he was well out of the territory of Jezebel. Words are very powerful and they can so easily wound, bruise and crush the spirit.

We read in Proverbs 18:21 that:

'Death and life are in the power of the tongue.'

Many children have been crushed in their spirits through the harsh words of parents, for their opinions are so important to the child. If they have said words such as: 'You are no good,' 'You're hopeless,' 'You are ugly, no one will want to marry you,' 'You are pathetic,' then the child will believe those words, causing them to go straight into the spirit bringing deep wounding. In this area of words bad news can have the same effect:

'And it shall be that when they say to you, Why do you sigh? that you shall answer, Because of the tidings, When it comes, ... and every spirit will faint.' (Ezekiel 21:7)

This was true of Jacob's spirit, when he heard the bad tidings concerning his son Joseph:

'I will go down to Sheol (the place of the dead) to my son mourning,' (Genesis 37:35)

and it was only when the good news came, (that Joseph was still alive) that we are told:

'the spirit of Jacob their father revived (and warmth and life returned).'

Functions Impaired

The function which is impaired when a spirit is crushed is that it becomes unable to comfort, sustain or empower their own, or other people's body and soul. However those with a crushed, bruised and heavy spirit can take courage, for Jesus has promised to restore and revive such people. He describes His role as being:

'to send forth as delivered those who are oppressed (who are downtrodden, bruised, crushed, and broken down by calamity).'

(Luke 4:18b)

Ministering to the Crushed Spirit

The story of Elijah is very helpful here, in the context of ministry, for it gives us a number of clues as to how to help those who are feeling downtrodden on the inside. One of the main lessons we can learn from this story is: be practical! Because the person's own spirit cannot strengthen or comfort their body, they will need to have someone draw alongside them, to do the job for them. God actually sent an angel to bake a cake for Elijah, which is very reminiscent of the time when Jesus provided a breakfast for the weary, crushed disciples (John 20). People who are crushed in spirit do not need another prayer meeting, or Bible study, however good these may be. It would be just one more burden! They need (as Scripture shows) to be loved and shown love, in as many practical ways as possible. The wisdom of God shows that there is a time when cake, bread and fish are more necessary than a portion of the Word.

So look for something that will encourage and comfort the person, depending on the reason and the response to the crushing. For one it may be a holiday, for another a teddy bear, for someone else a favoured pet. One lady whom we ministered to, was so fragile in spirit that the only practical thing that brought her any comfort was to lend her a family dog who took her for long walks! She was able to pour her heart out to the family pet, telling the animal secrets that no other human being knew, or ever needed to know. The walks and the listening ear brought a great deal of strength and comfort to her wounded spirit. If the reason for the crushing of the spirit was a burden too heavy to bear, and it is still present, there may be the need of another person's shoulder, to help bear the burden.

There comes a time, however, when they will need more than the practical. They will need to realise who they are in Christ, and begin to discover or rediscover, the strength which they have in Him. If you do this before the practical, it will have little or no effect. It needs to be done when they are stronger in their body and soul, which is exactly what God did with Elijah. Once he was fed, watered and had slept, God began to challenge him. In response to his cry of self-pity (that he was the only one who hadn't bowed the knee to Baal), God showed him that there were indeed:

> *'7,000 in Israel, all the knees that have not bowed to Baal and every mouth that has not kissed him.'* (1 Kings 18:18)

The person crushed in spirit will need help in renewing their vision. There comes a time when God says to Elijah, 'it is time to move on, I still have a purpose and a vision for you to accomplish.'

As well as being challenged as to who they are in Christ, they will need lots of encouragement and affection. Take plenty of time to feed the Word of God into them, reminding them that God will give them:

> *'the garment (expressive) of praise instead of a heavy, burdened, and failing spirit.'*
>
> (Isaiah 61:3)

If they are bruised and heavy in their spirits because of authoritarianism, strict leadership, or control, you will need to lift this away from them in prayer, and break, in the name of Jesus, any wrong bondings which may have been formed. For example, one man who came to us for ministry had to be set free from the power and influence of a Brethren leader, under whom he had served for a number of years. Because of the leader's strict legalistic lifestyle and type of control, he had thoroughly crushed this man's spirit and dominated his will. It was only when this bondage was broken that the man moved into a greater measure of freedom and was eventually able to become a leader in another church. This is not to say, however, that this is by any means true of other Brethren leaders, only that it happened in this instance.

As well as breaking any wrong bondings, you will also need to break the power of any harsh or abusive words which may have been spoken. Speak into them the positive in place of the negative. For example: 'You're not hopeless, you are a new creature in Christ Jesus, He loves you and created you for Himself.'

You can then begin to minister healing and deliverance, under the power of the Holy Spirit. He will bring thoughts, words or impressions to your spirit (to that intuitive part), in order that you can minister effectively and enable Him to give them:

> *'the garment (expressive) of praise instead of a heavy, burdened, and failing spirit.'*
>
> (Isaiah 61:3)

Summary

1. Give **practical** comfort.
2. Build into them a **realisation** of who they are in Christ.
3. Give lots of **encouragement** and **affection**.
4. Help them to renew their **vision**.
5. Feed the **Word of God** into them.

6. Lift off **manipulation** and **control**.
7. Break the power of **words**.
8. Minister **healing** and **deliverance** under the guidance of the Holy Spirit.

Chapter 9

Areas of Damage – A Defiled Spirit

The writer to the Corinthians exhorts:

> *'Let us cleanse ourselves from everything that contaminates and defiles body and spirit.'*
>
> (2 Corinthians 17:1)

It is not only the body that can become dirty and unclean, but the spirit also. It can pick up dirt, mud and filth, just as surely as the human body. When that happens we cannot communicate with God in the way we were meant to, and because of the filthiness of our spirits we cannot communicate with each other very clearly either. Everything becomes distorted.

The person with a defiled spirit will have a distinct lack of awareness of the presence of God, resulting in difficulty in staying in tune with Him. More likely than not there will be an interference with worship and a desire to run from praise. One lady we were ministering to was virtually unable to stay in the presence of God's people when they were worshipping. She inevitably, 'took to her heels' and ran, unable to bear the Glory of God. The more defilement there is, the harder it will be for the person to stay whilst worship is taking place.

If there is a defilement of spirit there may be an interest in, or a drawing towards, the occult. One young girl of thirteen, brought up in lovely Christian family (although adopted) had, when she became a teenager, a distinct interest in Tarot cards and the Ouija board. We were called in to minister when she was on the point of suicide. The Ouija board kept speaking one word to her continually: 'death'. On investigation we found that her mother had been into the occult and this seemed to have resulted in passing on to the child a generational defilement of spirit. Exodus 20:5 talks about God:

> *'visiting the iniquity of the fathers upon the children to the third and fourth generation of those who hate Me.'*

There may also be a sense of unwholeness in the spirit, especially if there have been any ungodly sexual relationships. (We will look more closely at this area when we consider the causes of a defiled spirit.)

Causes of a Defiled Spirit

One of the prime causes of our spirit becoming dirty or defiled is that each one of us is a sinner and therefore we will pick up dirt, dust or filth on a regular basis. We need to learn to keep a short account with God concerning our sin, continually, in a state of repentance, looking to Him for forgiveness and cleansing. John's letter reminds us that:

> *'If we (freely) admit that we have sinned and confess our sins, He is faithful and just (true to His own nature and promises) and will forgive our sins (dismiss our lawlessness) and (continuously) cleanse us from all unrighteousness.'*　　　　　　(1 John 1:9)

Another cause (as we have seen) is an involvement with the occult, either their own or generational. We have found in a number of instances, that where previous members of the family have been involved in other religions or freemasonry, there is often a confusion in the spirit, thus when reading Scripture the mind may become very confused or sleepy. What is happening? I believe that the defilement of the spirit, due to false worship, has resulted in confusing the mind or the body. Any form of idolatry can, according to Scripture, defile the spirit, as Paul writes to the Corinthians concerning idol worship:

> *'What agreement (can there be between) a temple of God and idols? For we are the temple of the living God: even as God said, I will dwell in and with and among them and will walk in and with and among them, and I will be their God, and they shall be My people. So, come out from*

among (unbelievers), and separate (sever)
yourselves from them, says the Lord, and touch
not (any) unclean thing.'

(2 Corinthians 6:16, 17)

Luke, in the book of Acts, picks up the same
theme and records that the apostles and the elders
agreed that they should send word to the Gentiles
to:

'abstain from and avoid anything that has
been polluted by being offered to idols.'

(Acts 15:20)

Thus we see that contact with any form of idolatry can cause pollution and defilement.

Because sexual intercourse is more than just a
physical act, Paul writes to the Corinthians:

'do you not know and realize that when a man
joins himself to a prostitute, he becomes one
body with her? The two, it is written, shall
become one flesh.'

Therefore ungodly or perverted sexual bondings
can be another source of defilement. Whatever is in
the human spirit of one person has the potential of
transferring into the spirit of the other person, thus
defiling them. This is especially true if one of the
partners has been into the occult. According to
Ezekiel prostitution defiles and pollutes. Referring
to prostitution he says:

> *'And the Babylonians came to her into the bed of love, and they defiled her with their evil desire.'*
>
> (Ezekiel 23:17)

Paul urged the Christians to come out from among unbelievers, because he knew that certain company can defile the spirit, as do bitter roots. There is the admonition in Scripture not to let any bitter root spring up and so defile many (Hebrews 12:15).

Those involved with ministering to others need to be aware that ministry situations can also cause defilement and pollution to their spirit. There are a number of reasons for this: it may be that they enter ministry without being prepared, or that there is an area of weakness in their own lives, or maybe are actively into unconfessed sin themselves. It is very important that those involved in ministry walk cleanly before the Lord; learn how to take spiritual protection and be able to use spiritual hygiene when necessary. Because people involved with prayer ministry are usually folk with very sensitive spirits, it is all too easy for them to become contaminated by the 'dirt' which they are praying into, if they forget to prepare their own hearts first.

Functions Impaired

The functions impaired because of a defiled spirit are: the conscience becomes darkened and it has difficulty distinguishing between right and wrong; judgement over sin becomes confused;

communication with God is hindered especially in worship (like interference on radio waves); and the faculties of revelation and intuition are seriously distorted:

> *'Now we are looking in a mirror that gives only a dim (blurred) reflection.'* (1 Corinthians 13:12)

The same principle applies to the human spirit if it is dirty and unclean.

Ministering to the Defiled Spirit

The person needs to be led to a place of repentance concerning any known sin or occult activity which they have been into. If they know of any generational sin they will need to confess it on behalf of their ancestors, just as Ezra (Ezra 9:5–15) and Nehemiah did:

> *'Yes, I and my father's house have sinned,'*
> (Nehemiah 1:6)

asking the Lord to take away the consequences of that sin.

If there have been any ungodly sexual bondings these will need breaking, and the consequences dealt with through prayer. The human spirit will need to be cleansed from any wrongful spirit contamination, remembering that it is the Word of God that cleanses:

'You are cleansed and pruned already, because of the word which I have given you.' (John 15:3)

Throughout the ministry to the person with a defiled spirit, the Holy Spirit will usually bring words of knowledge, wisdom or discernment to the person ministering. It is important to allow Him to take the lead and to remember that, as in every ministry situation, there is no technique, only the Holy Spirit as the leader. Always be aware of the need to look for and deal with the demonic if, and when, necessary.

Summary

1. Lead them to **repantance** for their own, or generational sin.
2. Break any ungodly **bondings**.
3. **Cleanse** the spirit from all defilement.
4. Minister Healing and Deliverance under the guidance of the **Holy Spirit**.

Chapter 10

Areas of Damage –
A Broken Spirit

In the area of being wounded in the human spirit, this is the most serious condition of all. The people who are walking around with a broken spirit are in a very critical condition indeed. Job asserts:

> *'My Spirit is broken, my days are spent (snuffed out); the grave is ready for me.'* (Job 17:1)

Unfortunately many people assume they are emotionally ill, when really the problem is not in their emotions but in their spirits. This is probably because they feel so sad and grief-stricken, they think it must be emotionally linked. However the sadness and sorrow are primarily the 'cause' of the brokenness in spirit, and not the 'result'. As the writer to Proverbs tells us, the reason for a broken spirit is that:

> *'By sorrow of heart the spirit is broken.'*

I believe that there are more people walking around with a broken spirit who are trying to get healed in their emotions, than we have realised. If the problem is in the spirit, then that is the wound that needs healing. To simply minister into the emotions will only deal with the symptoms and not with the root. However the symptoms do give us a clue as to who may be suffering from this dreadful disease.

What are the symptoms, then, of the one whose spirit is broken? Usually there are a number of physical signs, such as sadness of face. As the writer of Proverbs remarks:

> *'A glad heart makes a cheerful countenance,'*
> (Proverbs 15:13)

so conversely, we could conclude that a sad heart makes a sorrowful countenance. This, of course, is borne out by experience (apart from those people who try to put a cheerful face on at all costs) and usually it is very costly! Very often the broken in spirit will show signs of premature ageing: stooped shoulders, greying hair, dragging steps. Why is that? Well according to Proverbs:

> *'A broken spirit dries up the bones.'*
> (Proverbs 17:22)

The spirit cannot do its job function of strengthening and empowering the body and soul because of its brokenness, and thus becomes stooped and weary. I walked behind a lady and gentleman last week, who by their whole body appearance and facial expressions, were obviously the recent hearers of bad news. Their broken spirit was so evident to all with the eyes to see. Having prayed with a number of people with arthritis (many of whom have suffered from deep, deep grief way back in their past), the statement in Scripture that a broken spirit dries up the bones is not surprising. That is not to say, however, that **all** arthritis is caused by grief or a broken spirit.

Sleeplessness is another physical symptom:

> *'His (Nebuchadnezzar) spirit was troubled and agitated and his sleep went from him.'*
>
> (Daniel 2:1)

It is not unusual for the broken in spirit to toss and turn most of the night and then fall asleep just as the day dawns. Constant and seemingly inappropriate weeping may be a sign as well, like the lady who had an horrific accident when she was three years old. She would find herself crying for no apparent purpose. One of the reasons, I believe, was that when she was three, alongside bones being broken, her spirit was broken also.

Resorting to anorexic or bulimia type of behaviour can also be a sign of deep grief and a broken spirit.

Another physical manifestation would be the presence of frequent and constantly changing physical infirmities:

> *'The strong spirit of a man sustains him in bodily pain or trouble, but a weak and broken spirit who can raise up or bear?'*

(Proverbs 18:14)

Sometimes people are cruelly labelled as hypochondriacs, when really the physical pain and illnesses are simply the symptoms, the outcome or the result of their broken spirit.

There will also be a number of emotional symptoms, a sense of continual sorrow, sadness, despair and grief or deep and bitter anger leading to a state of rebellion. The person may be, or may become, very dependent and fearful. Often there will be a sense of hopelessness and desolation. Some have described their feelings as **an inner rawness**, a **'bleeding on the inside'** an ache within which gets almost healed, then the pain starts again, like a physical wound with the scab continually being knocked off. Often there is an over-sensitivity, a prickliness about the person. There will probably be an **inability to trust** anyone, for they might hurt you badly again and thus add to your pain. They may have what I would call a 'closed spirit', just as Jacob had, when his sons told him that Joseph was alive:

> *'He (Jacob) refused to be comforted and said, I will go down to Sheol (the place of the dead) to my son mourning. And his father wept for him.'*

(Genesis 37:35)

Very often there will be a deep insecurity and finally a longing for death.

One Christian gentleman (the life and soul of any party) courted his wife from a very early age and was married to her for over forty years. When she died in her sixties, he was so overcome with grief that it caused his spirit to break. This resulted in him grieving himself to death within a very short time.

Causes of a Broken Spirit

The main cause of a broken spirit is that of any loss situation which causes deep sorrow. As we have seen already:

> *'By sorrow of heart the spirit is broken.'*
> (Proverbs 15:13)

Genesis 37:33–35 tells of the deep brokenness of spirit of the patriarch Jacob on hearing of the supposed death of Joseph:

> *'And Jacob tore his clothes, put on sackcloth, and mourned many days for his son.'*
> (Genesis 37:34)

Later in the story we are told:

> *'When he (Jacob) saw the wagons which Joseph had sent to carry him, the spirit of Jacob their father revived.'* (Genesis 45:27)

Thus the loss of people one has loved, either by death, separation or divorce, can break the spirit. However it isn't only the loss of a loved one; the loss of a job or a career can have the same effect, as can the loss of important material things, loss of status or even the removal or loss of a ministry. We prayed with one Pastor who, because he had been betrayed by someone in his fellowship, had eventually lost his congregation. He was absolutely devastated and his spirit was truly broken. We have also ministered to many other Pastors who in their hearts fear failure, and are already beginning to show signs of a fracture in their spirits.

As well as loss or potential loss situations, other causes of a broken spirit would be pre-natal and birth traumas, such as a breech birth, caesarean, or attempted but unsuccessful abortions. If, as we have noted, babies in the womb can pick up in their spirits what is happening in, and around them, then an attempted abortion would surely have a devastating effect. Any present day traumas, such as violent or sudden accidents, acrimonious divorce etc. can also bring deep sorrow and break the spirit.

Rejection at any point is one of the most likely reasons for a person developing a broken spirit and there are a number of 'key times' when this can happen: during any traumatic pre-birth or birth experiences, for example; if a child is conceived in rape or anger, or is the wrong sex at birth, if a child is abandoned by meaningful people, for instance; adopted or fostered children; or those who have lost a parent through death, at an early age; if a child is rejected by their peer group during puberty or their teen years; any life experiences which bring rejection, for example; wives or husbands who have been deserted by their spouses. All of these times and experiences can spell rejection to the inner person and cause a deep brokenness of spirit.

Another cause would be that of betrayal, especially by friends. One lady, who had been recently divorced, said that the cause of her broken spirit was not her husband's unfaithfulness, but the betrayal by her best friend. That was the cut which went the deepest. Any disappointments, unfulfilled dreams or dashed hopes, break the spirit. For example we are told that Hannah was a woman *'of sorrowful spirit'* (1 Samuel 1:15) because of her childlessness. Many women with whom I have prayed and ministered to, because of the barrenness of their wombs, have needed deep ministry into their broken spirits also. These wounds go very deep. If someone gets to a certain age and they feel that life has passed them by, that they will never fulfil their dreams and ambitions, or children leave home against the parents wishes, then hearts may be filled with sadness and sorrow and thus cause the spirit to be broken.

Another major cause of a broken spirit is that of abuse: physical, verbal, emotional or sexual abuse will cause a deep rift in the spirit of the victim, which often leaves the person totally broken on the inside. Having ministered into many, many, people who have been sexually abused, I am so grateful that the Lord included this subject in the Scriptures. There are a number of instances, but I refer to only one, which is the story of Tamar, who was sexually abused by her brother Amnon. After he had raped her, he rejected her, calling his servant and saying:

> *'Put this women out of my presence now, and bolt the door after her.'*　　(2 Samuel 13:17)

Later we read that Tamar wandered around:

> *'a desolate women.'*　　(2 Samuel 13:20)

She was totally broken in spirit, as we can see from that very descriptive word, 'desolation', which means solitary, uninhabited, ruinous, neglected, barren, forlorn, disconsolate and wretched.

Functions Impaired

The function which is most damaged here is the almost total breakdown of communication. Because the spirit is broken it cannot feed life, strength, encouragement or comfort to the person concerned, or to anyone else. It has difficulty communicating with God or receiving from the Holy Spirit in the whole area of the intuition or the conscience. Thus the broken in spirit behaves like a broken car, with all primary and secondary functions seriously malfunctioning!

Ministering to the Broken Spirit

First of all the deep wounds need to be acknow-ledged, both by the one ministering and by the person themselves. It is much easier, and more common, to do this if a person has a physical wound, but those with a wounded, broken spirit, need sympathy and acknowledgement also. Some-times the recognition of the problem and the source of the pain is in itself a major step towards healing. As with any physical wound, there will need to be a time of probing and cleansing. Most sufferers will find this a very difficult process and will want to postpone or delay the 'operation' for as long as pos-sible. Gently, but firmly, they will need to be brought to face the issues and the cause of the brokenness. They need to see that for true and last-ing healing to take place, the wound needs to be exposed. It is vitally important that the person ministering be like a qualified surgeon, digging gently but deeply into the wound, continually exposing it to the Holy Spirit. The reason for the probing is in order that any infections which are there may be taken out of the wound and we are not therefore guilty of the accusation that:

> *'They have healed the wound of the daughter of My people only lightly and slightingly, saying, Peace, peace, when there is no peace.'*
>
> (Jeremiah 8:11)

The infections will vary tremendously, depending

on the reason for the wounding. As you wield the knife, under the direction of the Holy Spirit, you may find hardness of heart, resentment, deep anger, bitterness and unforgiveness. Very often during ministry, people will say such words as: 'Why did God let that happen to me?' 'If He is so good, how come this awful thing happened?' 'Why did my marriage fail? We both prayed and loved the Lord.' 'Why have my children gone off the rails?' The words need to be spoken out and the bitterness behind them recognised and released.

When all the infections have been drained away at the Cross, then there will probably be many forgiveness issues to deal with. There will be some people they will need to forgive, including many in the Body of Christ who have walked past their pain because it was on the inside. They may even be holding a grudge against God Himself, if they feel that He has been the cause of their sorrow. Of course with our minds we know God is not guilty, but if the person feels it in their spirit, then they need to choose to forgive even the Lord Himself. One of the key people they will need to express forgiveness towards will be themselves, for many of them will feel guilty for 'not being stronger', 'for not coping better' etc.

Bitter roots need to be confronted and removed. Many of these will be linked with inner vows which they have made at the time of the wounding. 'I will never give myself to a person again', 'I have failed', 'I am useless', 'God cannot possibly use me again'.

Such bitter roots need exposing and removing through the power of the Holy Spirit.

The person needs to be encouraged to turn from their own solutions, which may have been many and varied: sexual satisfaction as with the woman at the well (John 4); the desire for retaliation; a wanting to get revenge for the hurt and pain which eats away on the inside; a craving for food and comfort eating; a desire for new clothes in order to try and develop a new image and hopefully a new lifestyle; the use of escape mechanisms, such as sport or television taken to excess; becoming a workaholic in order to mask the pain or turning to drugs and alcohol. Some people develop a 'Back to the wall' syndrome (no one is going to hurt me again), or even use other people as a solution, and dependence may then become an issue.

Once the infections, bitter roots, and the person's own solutions have been exposed and dealt with, then we need to look for and minister into the roots and causes of the wounding. This can only be done effectively under the guidance and gifting of the Holy Spirit. If you have a car that is totally broken down, you send for the best mechanic possible to mend it. If you can get the original creator, so much the better. As we have seen, it is God Himself who formed the spirit of man within him (Zechariah 12:1), and it is the Holy Spirit who brings that spirit to life, when it is dead in trespasses and sin (John 6:63). Therefore it would make sense to call upon Him when the spirit needs fixing and healing. Jesus Himself affirms at the beginning of His ministry that He was anointed to:

> *'preach the good news (the Gospel) to the poor; He has sent Me to announce release to the captives and recovery of sight to the blind, to send forth as delivered those who are oppressed (who are downtrodden, bruised, crushed, and broken down by calamity).'* (Luke 4:18)

So we see that Father, Son and Holy Spirit are involved in the creation and healing of the human spirit, which is why we need Him to be present whenever we are ministering into this area.

Once the roots of the brokenness have been exposed and dealt with (either by inner healing prayers, deliverance or both) then the person will need lots of after-care and affection. There is a real need for godly people, at this point of ministry, who will take time to build up and strengthen those who are recuperating, feeding the truth of God into them, the truth that they are special, that there is hope, that God still has a purpose for them. They will need lots of tender expressions of love from the Body of Christ, a pouring into them of the *'balm of Gilead'*, a deep acceptance of them as people on the road to healing.

Summary

1.   An **acknowledgement** of the wound.
2.   **Infections** to be removed from the wound.

3. A **cleansing** of the wound.
4. A turning from their own **solutions**.
5. A need to uncover the **roots**.
6. Minister under the guidance of the **Holy Spirit**.
7. Feed in encouragement, love and acceptance.

Conclusion

Only Jesus can heal the broken hearted. That's His job description, but as part of the Body of Christ, it's also yours! Those who are called to minister healing in the name of Jesus need to recognize that some people for whom they pray will be wounded not only in their bodies and souls but also in their human spirits. We pray with Paul that those we meet in the Body of Christ will become sound in: *'spirit and soul and body'* (1 Thessalonians 5:23) and in order for that to happen, we need to learn how to co-operate with the Holy Spirit, in order that they may become whole.

One of the most beautiful qualities of the Holy Spirit is the one which I mentioned previously, concerning His ability to draw alongside the one with a wounded spirit, and align Himself with them. Thus the Holy Spirit and the human spirit become engaged like cogs in a wheel. When this happens, He does for the timid, the imprisoned, the defiled, the crushed and the broken, what they cannot do for themselves. He Himself performs and undergirds the job functions of the human spirit until eventually the person comes to a place of wholeness and healing. This is the meaning of the title *'Paracletos'*.

Do you remember what His and the human spirit's job functions are? To **communicate** life; to **comfort** those who mourn; to bring **strength** to the weak; to **reveal** the Father's heart; to bring **conviction** of sin; to take part in **creative** activities; to bring **hope** to the hopeless; to pour **affection** on the affectionless; to grant **security** to the fearful; to bring **release** to the imprisoned; to **revive** the fainting and to enable God's plans to be brought to fruition, thus bringing in the Kingdom of God.

To be a part of the ministry to the wounded human spirit is a tremendous responsibility, but it is also a wonderful privilege.